Men-at-Arms • 33

The US Cavalry

John Selby • Illustrated by Michael Roffe
Series editor Martin Windrow

First published in Great Britain in 1972 by Osprey Publishing,
Midland House, West Way, Botley, Oxford OX2 0PH, UK
44-02 23rd St, Suite 219, Long Island City, NY 11101, USA
Email: info@ospreypublishing.com

Transferred to digital print on demand 2010

First published 1972
3rd impression 2005

Printed and bound by PrintOnDemand-Worldwide.com, Peterborough, UK

A CIP catalogue record for this book is available from the British Library

ISBN: 978 1 84176 351 4

Series Editor: Martin Windrow

The Woodland Trust
Osprey Publishing is supporting the Woodland Trust, the UK's leading woodland conservation charity,
by funding the dedication of trees.

www.ospreypublishing.com

The Early Years, 1772-1848

The Polish count, Casimir Pulaski, who in 1777 became the first American chief of cavalry

The first commander of American cavalry was Count Casimir Pulaski. In 1772 Pulaski led a force in a fight for Polish freedom; but was defeated by the Russians, and had his estates confiscated. He escaped to France, and when he heard about the American rebellion against the British, saw Benjamin Franklin in Paris and offered his services to the rebels. Franklin gave him a letter of introduction to George Washington who placed him in command of the cavalry. At that time cavalrymen were used only as messengers, and for guard duties; but the aggressive Pole soon taught them how to charge.

On 11 September 1777, at Brandywine near Wilmington, Delaware, the British surrounded an American force; and Pulaski saved it from being completely annihilated by gathering small groups of cavalrymen to charge the encircling enemy, thus putting the British off balance.

Although superseded by General Stephen Moylan as Chief of Cavalry, Pulaski was allowed to raise

Stephen Moylan, who took over the Continental Cavalry at Valley Forge when Pulaski resigned in March 1778

3

Francis Marion, the 'Swamp Fox', whose cavalry captured Georgetown

Light Horse Harry Lee, whose cavalry fought at the Battle of Cowpens. His son was Robert E. Lee who became commander of the Confederate forces in the Civil War

and lead a force of 300 horsemen of his own. These were dressed in uniforms of varied design. Some who had served with the French wore parts of their French hussar uniform; three Poles, one of them Pulaski's cousin, were dressed in remnants of Polish uniform; and a number of Hessians were garbed as they had been when they arrived in America.

When the British landed at Egg Harbor, New Jersey, in October 1779, Pulaski's force attacked them and cut them to pieces; but a year later he was mortally wounded by a splinter from a British shell outside Savannah, Georgia.

Another early cavalry leader of note was Francis Marion, 'the Swamp Fox'. Marion led three South Carolina regiments of horse, who wore scarlet coats, and in their hats had silver pins inscribed 'Liberty or Death'. Marion's troopers frequently entered a fight on foot, only using their horses to reach the battlefield. They won a great reputation by making frequent surprise raids, and because of this are considered to be the first Special Forces of the United States Army. One of their most notable achievements was the capture of Georgetown, South Carolina, in 1781.

With the advent of the British Colonel Tarleton, a proper full-scale cavalry engagement took place in 1781 at Cowpens, 200 miles north of the east coast port of Savannah. Outstanding here on the American side was Colonel William Washington, a cousin of the General. Sent in against Tarleton's flank, Washington's squadron attacked with such élan that they threw the British into confusion. In the end the British suffered 830 casualties to 93 for the Americans, so the latter can justly claim a victory.

Another leading cavalryman of the period was Henry Lee, the father of Robert E. Lee of Civil War fame. Lee constantly attacked the British lines of communications, and in a space of less than two months captured five British posts and took 1,100 prisoners. Finally, at the British surrender at Yorktown in October 1781, the American cavalry of 100 dragoons combined well with the more numerous allied French cavalry and contained the British mounted forces effectively.

After Cornwallis's surrender the American cavalry almost ceased to exist. In 1798, owing to the fear of war with France, Congress authorized the enlargement of the last remaining company of dragoons into a regiment. The men of the new regiment were dressed in green coats with white buttons and facings, and wore cocked hats bearing a black cockade and eagle badge. When the war scare passed, the regiment of dragoons was cut to two troops; only to be enlarged again into two regiments during the 1812–15 war against the British, for which, unfortunately, there is no record of engagements. The dragoons were completely disbanded in 1821, revived in 1833, and from then on established permanently. The new dragoons emerged from a force of irregular Mounted Rangers embodied to settle Indians in reserves in the West. After this task had been satisfactorily completed most of the Ranger officers were transferred to the new 1st Dragoons. There were several noteworthy figures, including Philip St George Cooke, later to become a distinguished cavalryman, and Jefferson Davis the future President of the Confederation.

The 1st Dragoons were mustered near St Louis in 1834. Under Colonel Dodge, also from the Rangers, they marched 400 miles south-west to Fort Gibson on the Arkansas River, and then west into Comanche country. Their object was to visit and impress the tribes who were to be the neighbours of the Indians moved there from the East.

The expedition had been planned for May with the good pastures; but owing to recruiting and equipping difficulties the column did not set off until June. The cavalry formed the advance part of a force under General Leavenworth, and the late start was very nearly the cause of destroying them early on. It turned dreadfully hot, and the humid air of the Mississippi basin caused the troopers to suffer severely from heat exhaustion. To this was added fever caused by drinking the impure water found in the prairie water-holes, so that after a journey of only eighty miles half the men collapsed from the heat or dysentery.

When the rear party came up a camp was established for the sick men and unsound horses. With the good May grass gone, however, the latter were slow to recover. In spite of all these difficulties, after a short halt, the undaunted Colonel Dodge led forward 200 troopers on those horses capable of continuing. They were followed by General Leavenworth and some of the infantry.

The General was soon in trouble. First he fell sick with fever, and then when he had recovered he was thrown from his horse while hunting buffalo, and killed. Dodge, however, unaware of his superior's death, pushed on, passing through brush country where in places the undergrowth was so dense that it had to be hacked down to make a path.

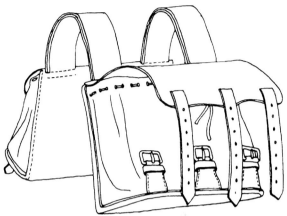

Russet leather saddlebags of the Revolution, for personal belongings, including combs, hoof pick and nosebag for the horse. One suspension strap passed over the saddle, the other just behind the saddle

When they reached the open prairie beyond the brush they entered territories inhabited by the Osages and Kiowas. These two tribes were carrying on a desultory war with each other; but the presence of the long blue column of disciplined troopers marching through their country had a good effect. Not only did the Indians agree to stop their warlike activities temporarily, but they also said they would visit Fort Gibson in the autumn to parley.

Dodge now decided to return. Reaching the rearguard, whom he found enlarging the sick camp for more invalids, and hearing of Leavenworth's death, he took over command and led the effectives back to Fort Gibson, leaving the ailing men and horses to come along behind at a slower rate. Although the casualties were severe, being 90 out of a total cavalry force of 600, the results were not unsatisfactory. Soon after Dodge's return on 24 August the Osages and Kiowas started coming in to treat for peace, and were followed by other tribes. What was more, the Indians transferred from the East were left in peace by their neighbours sufficiently long to allow them to settle down in their new and rather disappointing country.

There followed several other expeditions westwards over the plains. One, led by Colonel Dodge again, was from Fort Leavenworth to the Arkansas valley to visit the Comanches. They found the area relatively peaceful, and this although the Cheyennes were stealing the ponies of the Comanches. Meanwhile Colonel Stephen Watts Kearny, who had taken part in the first expedition, established Fort Des Moines further north in Sioux country. At this time the possession of Oregon on the west coast was in dispute with Britain, and, from Des Moines, Kearny made a noteworthy exploratory march with 300 dragoons westwards up the Oregon trail as far as South Pass, over the Rockies, in the present State of Wyoming. Including the return journey, Kearny and his dragoons covered about 1,000 miles. On the way back they met 3,000 settlers moving westwards up the Oregon Trail. Later, when the great gold rushes began, the cavalry were required to guard passengers on the trail from attacks by Sioux aroused to resentment by the sight of the numerous intruders.

The charge of General Grant at the Battle of Shiloh

In 1836 another mounted regiment, the 2nd Dragoons, was authorized by Congress primarily for use against the Seminole Indians of Florida, who were making settlers' lives hazardous. It was planned to move the Seminoles to reservations in the West, but the task was found extremely difficult. For ten years or so the Seminoles played hide-and-seek in the Florida swamps and defied efforts to dislodge them. The 2nd Dragoons, to their disgust, spent most of their time dismounted,

wading through swamps or poling canoes through the Everglades. The war was finally ended in 1842 when Colonel Worth defied precedent, and, in the trying summer months considered unsuitable for active operations, took his 8th Infantry into the depths of the Everglades and destroyed the Seminole hide-outs. Before this, however, in the autumn of 1841, the 2nd Dragoons had been ordered to Arkansas.

The field uniform of the 2nd Dragoons during the Seminole War was a dark blue jacket trimmed with yellow, a blue service cap with a yellow band and light blue breeches with yellow stripes.

About this time the settlers in Texas were seeking independence from their Mexican overlords, and in 1845 the United States annexed Texas. Following this came the Mexican War of 1845–48. During the war Colonel Kearny led 100 dragoons to Santa Fé, and then striking west over the southern end of the chain of the Rockies, proceeded down the valley of the Gila into California where there were already detachments of the U.S. Navy, some marines, and a force under General Frémont. The rest of the 1st Dragoons and the 2nd Dragoons were in the force under General Zachary Taylor which crossed the Rio Grande and invaded Mexico proper from the north. Finally in 1846 a new regiment was formed, the Mounted Rifles, with distinctive green trimming on their blue jackets appropriate for riflemen. This regiment was formed to guard the Oregon Trail, but was quickly diverted to Mexico, where it won great distinction serving with General Winfield Scott when he landed a force on the east coast at Veracruz and marched inland to capture Mexico City.

California and New Mexico to the south were far from the centre of Mexico and nearer to the United States, from where they could be reached by the Santa Fé Trail. When war was declared it was decided not only to invade Mexico proper but to conquer California and New Mexico. Besides troops already in California, several hundred mounted men including the 1st Dragoons, a battery of artillery and two companies of infantry were assembled to move against New Mexico and California via the Santa Fé Trail. After occupying Santa Fé without much difficulty Colonel Kearny moved on at the head of 300 dragoons towards

California. While still in the valley of the Rio Grande he met the frontiersman Kit Carson riding east with despatches announcing the surrender of California by the Mexicans to the American troops there. Kearny then sent back all his wagons to Santa Fé, as well as 200 of the troopers. With his supplies packed on mule back and two twelve-pounders, a highly reluctant Kit Carson as guide, and 100 troopers dressed in blue flannel breeches and shirts, mostly mounted on mules, he headed due west from the Rio Grande across the southern end of the chain of the Rockies in a dash for the coast. Meanwhile the despatches had been turned over to a substitute rider.

Guided by Carson the dragoons passed the old Santa Rita copper mines, and coming to the headwaters of the Gila River followed its westward course to the confluence with the Colorado River. The dragoons hit the river at a point high above sea level where it flowed swift and clear through good grazing land for their mounts. Though it was deep in Apache country, a force of 100 well-armed dragoons had nothing to fear.

Indeed the Apaches, when encountered, proved friendly and willing to trade. In places the going was tough, and the wheeled twelve-pounders found the boulder-strewn canyons particularly difficult to cross, and were often left behind. On leaving the mountains they learned that the Mexicans in California had risen against the Americans who were now in difficulties, so Kearny pushed his men on by forced marches towards San Diego. Short of this town the column encountered some Mexican lancers and Kearny ordered his men to charge them. This nearly proved their undoing, for the Mexicans having first retreated, turned and charged back, killing 19 and wounding 15. Kearny and the remainder extricated themselves with difficulty, assisted by marines sent up from the coast. A few days later they marched into San Diego. Together, the troops in California, Kearny's column, and the Mormon battalion which had followed him on a route south of the Gila, then subdued California. New Mexico had already been placed under the control of the United States.

General Sickles on a reconnaissance in the Potomac, from a contemporary newspaper

7

Meanwhile, the 2nd Dragoons and the rest of the 1st Dragoons had joined General Zachary Taylor's force which was attacking Mexico from across the Rio Grande. In May 1846, before the Rio Grande was reached, 'Rough and Ready' Taylor, as he was called, routed the Mexican cavalry at the Battle of Palo Alto with his infantry and artillery alone. Next day, however, while still short of the river, a splendid cavalry action took place. After sending his wounded to the coast, and leaving his wagon train under guard at Palo Alto, General Taylor moved forward with his army and came up with the Mexican force at Resaça. A deep ravine separated the two armies, but a road went round its eastern end. Behind the ravine and beside the road were placed the Mexican guns. When Mexican fire had halted the advance of the American infantry, General Taylor ordered Captain May to charge with his squadron of 2nd Dragoons round the east flank of the ravine against the guns guarding the road, while an American battery gave covering fire. This was just what Captain May liked doing, and he immediately thundered forward with his dragoons through the smoke, carrying the guns and scattering the Mexican infantry supporting them. And not only did he capture the guns. Rallying his scattered troopers under severe fire from Mexican infantry who had not been broken, he seized and carried off General la Vega himself. The American infantry then crossed the ravine and poured down the road at the double-quick, and the battle was won. Mexican losses at Resaça exceeded 1,000 even before the routed army reached the Rio Grande, where drowning raised the toll. The Americans had 33 dead and less than 100 wounded.

After the battle, Taylor continued towards the Rio Grande, and reaching Fort Brown prepared to cross the river. His crossing was completed by 20 May 1846, and he next moved against Monterrey, the capital of Northern Mexico. General Worth, who had been promoted after his successful campaign against the Seminoles in Florida, was in command of the force attacking Monterrey, and had to assist him in his task the famous Texas Rangers.[1] Armed with rifles and Colts, mounted on wiry prairie mustangs, with outlandish dress and huge beards, and entering battle uttering horrible shrieks, they terrified the Mexicans. At

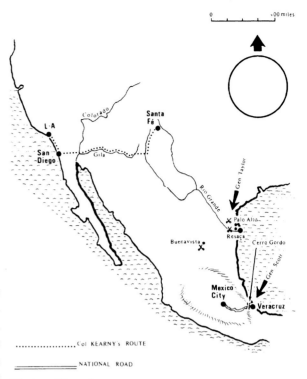

Mexican War, 1847

Monterrey they acted as Worth's shock troops. After making a wide encircling movement, they repelled a charge by Mexican lancers, and then dismounted and stormed the outer defences of the town. Finally, along with the rest of Worth's force, they fought from house to house inside. This was the worst sort of dismounted fighting. The houses were built Mexican style, flush and almost blind to the street, with tough adobe walls and iron grilles on the few small windows. It took a full week to blast the defenders off the rooftops and out from behind the adobe walls and herd them in the centre plaza of Monterrey.

With a long line of supply and communication to hold behind him and no clear idea of just what he was expected to do in Mexico, Taylor was glad to get the city on any terms. He therefore signed an eight-week armistice with General Pedro de Ampudia and allowed the Mexican soldiers to march out of the town. It is hard to see how he could have taken them prisoner, since they outnumbered his entire force; but President Polk and the Commanding General of the Army, Winfield Scott, were outraged at what he had done. Taylor was ordered to redeem himself by marching at once on Mexico City. But he demurred strongly, and suggested instead that the assault should be made from the sea via Veracruz, by the route, in fact, that Cortes had used to capture the Aztec capital. To this Scott eventually agreed.

Meanwhile, the Mexicans counter-attacked Taylor's forces which had reached Buenavista, south-west of Monterrey. Taylor had been reinforced, and among the troops which joined him from the north-west were two companies of the 1st Dragoons.

At Buenavista, Santa Ana attacked with 21,000 troops, against Taylor's 4,500; and the battle that followed lasted two days and was the bloodiest of the war. In the first stage a large force of Mexican lancers and infantry advanced, and pushed back the American militia who were facing them, in spite of some spirited charges by the Volunteer cavalry. The routed militia fled through the local ranch and got crammed in the alleys between its buildings, where they were beset by the Mexican cavalry. This serious situation was resolved by the regular dragoons. Led by the redoubtable Captain May they thundered into the masses in the alleys, not caring greatly whether they struck friend or foe, and drove off the Mexicans. May's charge proved to be the turning point of the battle. Immediately afterwards the whole American line began a general advance, which even the routed militia were prevailed upon to turn and join, and Santa Ana's army was defeated. May, already brevetted twice for stirring charges, was again uplifted – now becoming 'Colonel' to his friends although still receiving a captain's pay!

Some of Taylor's troops were now sent to reinforce General Winfield Scott's column advancing on Mexico City from Veracruz, and Taylor was ordered to hold on to the positions he had gained.

Scott's cavalry was at first limited to three companies of 1st Dragoons, six of 2nd Dragoons and the newly raised regiment of Mounted Riflemen; the latter, however, having unfortunately lost most of their horses on the sea voyage, had thus to serve on foot – a great humiliation for a cavalryman! The wealthy Phil Kearny – nephew of Colonel Stephen Watts Kearny who led the dragoons to California – had mounted, at his own expense, his company of 1st Dragoons on splendid greys. These fortunately survived the voyage.

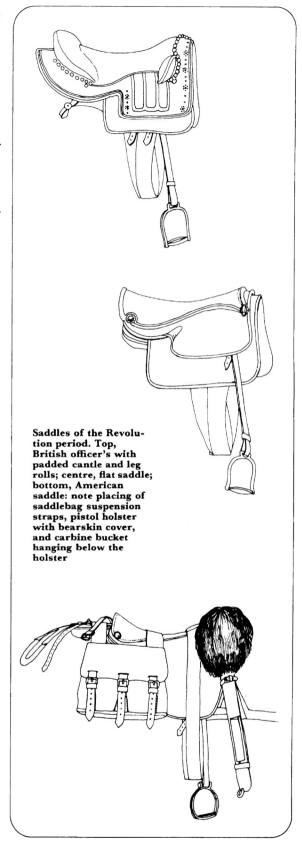

Saddles of the Revolution period. Top, British officer's with padded cantle and leg rolls; centre, flat saddle; bottom, American saddle: note placing of saddlebag suspension straps, pistol holster with bearskin cover, and carbine bucket hanging below the holster

The 7th New York Cavalry in their camp near Fairfax
Court House, Virginia, during the Civil War

After Veracruz had been taken by storm, the American forces marching inland were forced to fight a series of actions against Mexicans in defence positions on mountain barriers across the National Road. At one of these, the Cerro Gordo, General Scott carried out a model operation to clear the way. First, Captain Robert E. Lee[2] scouted round the Mexican flank and discovered a route to turn their position. Then, a flanking column swung round by it and cut the National Road while a frontal attack was keeping the Mexican defenders occupied. The Mounted Rifles played an important part in this battle, and not without loss, for they suffered 84 casualties.

After the battle enough horses were captured to mount two companies of Rifles, but the mounted men found that their infantry rifles were clumsy to use on horseback. After firing one shot they chose to charge the enemy rather than try to reload while mounted, which they could have done with a short cavalry carbine.

General Winfield Scott reached the outskirts of Mexico City in August 1847, and there defeated the Mexicans in two battles on successive days. In the second battle more horses were captured and more Rifles were able to revert to cavalry, this time some even doing so while the fighting was in progress. At one stage, Captain Phil Kearny at the head of his greys charged right through the enemy lines with twelve of his troops and captured a battery of enemy guns. Dismounted and isolated, they were so far ahead of their fellows that it seemed they must be lost; but the Mexicans proved too confused and bewildered to take advantage of the situation, and, quickly remounting, Kearny led his dragoons back through the Mexican ranks to safety, though one of his arms was shattered by a stray shot as he did so. This brave feat did not pass unnoticed by the Commander-in-Chief, for General Winfield Scott said later that he considered Kearny the bravest man he knew.

During the storming of Chapultepec castle, just before the entry of Mexico City, the Rifles charged the heights on foot, and next day received a striking acknowledgement by Scott, for it was their flag which was raised over the National Palace on its occupation. Also, when General Scott, escorted by Kearny's dragoons on their grey horses, passed along the ranks of the Mounted Rifles drawn up as guards along his path, he exclaimed: 'Brave Rifles! Veterans! You have been baptised in fire and blood and have come out steel.' These words were later taken by the Mounted Rifles, who became the 3rd U.S. Cavalry in July 1861, as their regimental motto.

With the capture of Mexico City the war came to an end. The Americans occupied the place for nearly nine months until the end of May 1848 when a treaty of peace was finally ratified.

The Civil War 1861-5

The Southern States had the advantage in the cavalry arm over the North at the beginning of the Civil War both as regards officers and men. Most of the experienced officers of the mounted service, including four full colonels of the five regular regiments, were Southerners, and resigned their commissions in the United States Army as their individual States seceded from the Union. They usually obtained commissions of a higher grade in the Confederate Army, and most of the senior officers quickly became generals. Among these were Robert E. Lee from the 2nd Cavalry, Joseph E. Johnston from the 1st Cavalry and J. E. B. Stuart from the Mounted Rifles. The rank and file of the South, many of them planters and farmers, were born horsemen with a natural flair for reconnaissance and long-range penetrations into enemy territory as well as for straightforward fighting. Many brought their own horses, and it was no rare thing for a Virginian gentleman to resign a commission in another arm to join his friends as an enlisted man in the cavalry. Many were well acquainted with the countryside which was to provide their battleground. They knew every country lane and woodland track, they had friends in every village, and their names were known to every farmer. 'We thought no more of riding through the enemy bivouacs than of riding round our fathers' farms,' was how they put it.

In the East, in the early days, the Federal cavalry were outmatched. Although there were exceptions from among those recruited from the Western States, throughout the North generally horsemanship was practically an unknown art. 'As cavalry,' says one of Bank's brigadiers, 'Ashby's men were greatly superior to ours. In reply to some orders I had given, my cavalry commander replied, "I can't catch them, sir; they leap fences and walls like deer; neither our men nor horses are so trained".' The Federal cavalry at this stage – they improved greatly later – were badly trained and unprepared for war. After Front Royal, Taylor records, 'The Federal horse was from New England, a section in which horsemanship was an unknown art, and some of the riders were strapped to their steeds. Ordered to dismount, they explained their condition and were given time to unbuckle.'

At the Battle of First Bull Run on 21 July 1861, the seven companies of regular cavalry attached to McDowell's army were under Colonel Palmer and covered the retreating Federal Army as they made their way over Stone Bridge to Centreville and Washington. They and Sykes's regular infantry were the only units which remained staunch up to the end. The next month, on 3 August, Congress passed a bill organizing all the mounted troops – dragoons, mounted riflemen and cavalry – into one branch, all to be called cavalry, and to be numbered by seniority, which produced the following:

Old Name	Date of Origin	New Name
1st Dragoons	1833	1st Cavalry
2nd Dragoons	1836	2nd Cavalry
Mounted Riflemen	1846	3rd Cavalry
1st Cavalry	1855	4th Cavalry
2nd Cavalry	1855	5th Cavalry
3rd Cavalry	1861	6th Cavalry

Cavalry yellow was designated as the colour of the new corps, and the facings of the other uniforms – orange for the dragoons and green for the mounted riflemen, to which all were strongly attached – were ordered to be changed; the usual permission, however, was given to wear out the uniforms on hand, and these achieved a remarkably long life.

Left
Turney Ashby first donned a military uniform in 1861, was killed in June 1862

Right
J. E. B. Stuart, the outstanding cavalry leader of the Civil War, and one of the greatest of any time

These six regular cavalry regiments were soon swamped and lost in a deluge of volunteer-mounted units which brought the strength of the Union cavalry to about 80,000 by the end of the war. Some States produced a very large number of volunteer regiments of cavalry; for example, Missouri had 23, Illinois 17, Pennsylvania 21 and New York 25. There were also six regiments of coloured Cavalry. In addition to these cavalry regiments, there were a number of mounted infantry regiments which were, to all intents and purposes, cavalry.

Although there were a multitude of skirmishes and many large-scale cavalry raids, cavalry battles were few and far between during the Civil War, the only one of significance being the encounter between General Pleasonton's Cavalry Corps and part of General J. E. B. Stuart's Corps at Brandy Station on 9 June 1863, a month after the Battle of Chancellorsville.

At this stage Lee persuaded the Confederate President Jefferson Davis and his cabinet that the war could best be pursued by carrying out an invasion of the North. He argued that if his invading army were to threaten the great towns in the North, a resulting clamour of the people against the war might very well force President Lincoln's administration to negotiate peace. At first this met with by no means unanimous approval in the South, but in the end he had his way. He thereupon began to move his army north-westwards up

the west bank of the Rappahannock towards the Shenandoah Valley with the intention of crossing the Potomac into Maryland in the neighbourhood of Harper's Ferry. This movement was to be screened by Stuart's cavalry holding the line of the Rappahannock River. Before the advance north began, both the opposing cavalry forces faced each other from opposite sides of the river in the neighbourhood of Rappahannock Station athwart the railway from Washington to Richmond, via Gordonsville: Stuart's divisions round and about Brandy Station on the west bank, Pleasonton's Corps nearer the river on the east.

'Jeb' Stuart had over 9,000 troopers in his divisions, all mounted, and twenty guns. They were in such excellent shape that he proudly invited Lee to inspect them. Lee was busy and declined, so on 5 June 1863 Stuart carried out his own full-scale dress review. The brigades marched past at the walk, and then at the gallop. A thirteen-gun salute was fired by the artillery for their Major-General. It was most impressive. The next day, Lee did come over to Stuart's headquarters at Brandy Station. The brigades prepared themselves, grumbling, for a repeat performance. Lee, however, only saw them pass by at the walk, before he went into conference with Stuart to discuss the coming Gettysburg campaign.

Hooker was still in command of the Army of the Potomac which had fared so badly at Chancellorsville. As always his information was poor. He believed Stuart had more than twice his actual number of troopers. A likely Confederate movement north had, however, been reported, so Hooker ordered Pleasonton's cavalry to cross the river and investigate what was happening.

Pleasonton divided his force into two parts, and his plan was for Buford's Division to cross the river at Beverley Ford north of the railway bridge, and Gregg's and Duffie's Divisions over Kelly's Ford well to the south. Russell's Division was to remain in reserve east of the river. After crossing, the northern and southern forces were to converge on Brandy Station.

After making their passage, Buford's leading brigade brushed with the 6th Virginian Cavalry, and news of the attack was sent back to Stuart. The Confederate regiment resisted staunchly, but numbers told, and it was forced back through the divisional artillery park. Here Buford's men had

the opportunity of capturing some guns, but there was too much confusion for the officers to organize their seizure, and the Confederate artillerymen were able to hook in and take them back to safety. Still, Jones's whole Brigade, which was now resisting the northern attack, was forced back towards Brandy Station, and the Union troops were able to begin an assault on Fleetwood Hill, to the north of it, where Stuart had his headquarters. Meanwhile, Gregg's leading brigade under Robertson crossed at Kelly's Ford, pushed back the pickets watching it, and drove up on Brandy Station from the south. Duffie's men, who crossed late, bore south-west, grappled with Wade Hampton's Brigade, occupied Stevensburg seven miles east of Culpeper, and sent a small force to reinforce Gregg's southern attack on Brandy Station. A tremendous struggle for Fleetwood Hill took place, and it changed hands several times. At one stage

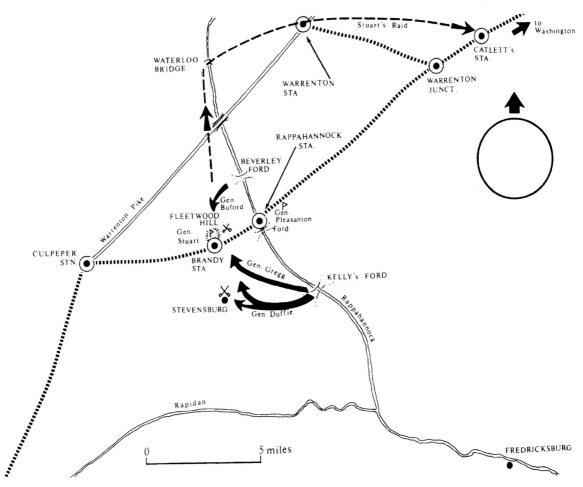

The encounter at Brandy Station

Stuart ordered the six-pounder by his head-quarters to open fire on Gregg's thousands of blue-clad riders charging towards him up the hill, only to be shelled back by several of Gregg's pieces. He quickly called up more regiments and guns to reinforce his forward positions. There followed an hours-long struggle for possession of the hill, with charge and counter-charge. In the

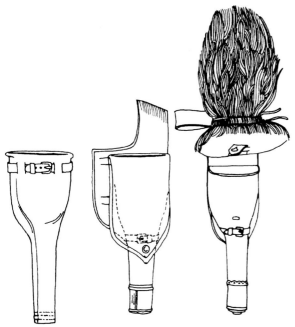

Holsters of the late eighteenth century. Left, one of the earliest types with a simple strap to attach to the pommel; centre, American holster with metal tip and broad suspension strap; right, the commonest form of holster with saddle thongs, bearskin cover, and brass tip

fighting, the 1st New Jersey and 6th Pennsylvania Cavalry particularly distinguished themselves in a long series of charges. However, the Southerners gained possession of the battlefield in the end. Duffie's Division was also defeated in the south and lost three guns, and on hearing that heavy foot reinforcements were coming up to help Stuart, Pleasonton ordered a retreat. This was carried out almost unmolested, and Buford recrossed at Beverley Ford, Gregg at Rappahannock Station, and Duffie at Kelly's Ford, without further loss.

The Confederates lost 523 to the Union losses of 936, but Stuart, nevertheless, is reckoned to have been 'caught napping', and was strongly criticized in the Southern press. Moreover, the Union cavalry achieved their mission of confirming Lee's coming move to the north by capturing despatches, and established, at last, a cavalry reputation for the North. McClellan wrote:[3] 'Up to that time confessedly inferior to the Southern horsemen, they gained on this day a confidence in themselves and in their commanders which enabled them to contest fiercely the subsequent battlefields.'

There were a number of cavalry leaders on both sides who carried out successful raids during the Civil War, particularly notable being Stuart, Forrest and Mosby for the Confederates, and Wilson for the Union.

After the Peninsular campaign, when Lee's forces were facing Pope's in central Virginia, at first on either side of the Rapidan River, and later across the Rappahannock, Stuart and his cavalry carried through several daring exploits. Lee decided to cross the Rapidan secretly and pass behind Pope's east flank, placing his army between Pope and Washington. During a preliminary cavalry reconnaissance Stuart was nearly caught by a Union patrol, and only escaped by making his horse leap a gate out of the garden of his temporary billet. Unfortunately, he left behind not only his famous plumed hat, but his despatch box containing Lee's dispositions. The Federals, thus warned, retreated back behind the Rappahannock, and the plan came to nothing. Later, however, while desultory actions were in progress along the line of the Rappahannock, Stuart got his own back. With 1,500 cavalry and two guns he moved north along the west bank of the Rappahannock, crossed at Waterloo Bridge, and took the direct road to Warrenton. He says: 'From this point I directed my march with a view to destroy the railroad bridge near Catlett's Station [on the railroad between Washington and Richmond via Gordonsville], and the telegraph line, and thus cut the enemy's line of communication. I had not proceeded far before a terrific storm set in which was a serious obstacle to the progress of artillery, and gave indications of continuing for a sufficient time to render the streams on my return impassable. We soon found ourselves in the midst of the enemy's encampments, on the darkest night I ever knew. Fortunately we captured at this critical moment a negro who had known me in Beverley, and who on recognizing me, gave the location of Pope's staff, baggage and horses, and offered to guide me to the spot.' Stuart's cavalry reached Catlett's Station, but found the railway bridge too difficult to destroy. However, having dealt with the telegraph and set the camp ablaze, they returned the way they had come with 300 prisoners including several officers, Pope's despatch book giving his strength and dispositions, and Pope's hat, his military cloak, and one of his uniform coats. Stuart was delighted with these. He hoped to trade them for his plumed hat.

Another outstanding Confederate cavalry leader was General N. B. Forrest. Forrest was almost completely unschooled. The only learning he acquired was, as he himself put it, what he got from 'leaning against the schoolhouse wall'. But he was shrewd enough to make a small fortune before the war, and appeared as a natural cavalry leader. It is reputed that Forrest described his own theory of war in the words: 'Git thar fustest with

the mostest.' It is doubtful if the self-educated Forrest spoke so ungrammatically in his mature years, but if this colourful statement was apocryphal, it nevertheless typified the basis of his tactics.

Forrest's greatest year was probably 1864, with two spectacular successes to his credit. Early in February, Sheridan marched due east from Vicksburg with the purpose of destroying the railroads radiating out from Meridian, and he ordered the cavalry force under Brigadier-General Smith to move down from the north to join him. It was known that Forrest's cavalry were operating north of Meridian, and Smith's task was to brush them aside, combine with Sherman in raids on the railroads around Selma east of Meridian, and destroy the Confederate arsenal there.

Smith started south on 11 February, and after three days came upon Forrest's force in a strong position which he declined to attack although he outnumbered Forrest by three to one. Then Smith fell back, and Forrest followed after him, and the two armies met at Okolona. There followed a

Nathan Bedford Forrest, an unlettered slave trader from Memphis ('Get thar fustest with the mostest' was his famous though apocryphal utterance), became a major-general in two years and employed his cavalry as mounted foot-soldiers

John Singleton Mosby, leader of Mosby's Raiders, a band of guerrillas who made daring and militarily unorthodox raids behind enemy lines

James Harrison Wilson, a major-general at 27. His troopers arrested Jefferson Davis at Irwinsville, Georgia

battle which lasted all day. When darkness approached, the Confederates were gaining the upper hand, and to allow time to strengthen his position, Smith ordered one of his regiments to make a mounted attack. The dismounted Confederate cavalry were more than a match for this. They opened a steady accurate fire and drove off the horsemen in confusion. This reverse took all the remaining fight out of Smith. He ordered a general retreat which culminated in a disorderly flight northwards. In the fighting, Forrest inflicted 400 casualties on his more numerous and better equipped foe for a loss of 150. Sherman, meanwhile, with his 20,000 men had been waiting at Meridian for the arrival of Smith and his cavalry. When they failed to join, he abandoned his project against Selma and returned to Vicksburg, bitterly disappointed. Forrest's small force had frustrated the operations of nearly 27,000 Northerners. It was, according to one of his contemporaries, 'the most glorious achievement of his career'.

Next Forrest moved north and attacked Fort Pillow on the Mississippi. He arrived there at dawn on 12 April 1864. Having driven back the outlying pickets into the fort, he worked his men into positions from which they could assault the place without coming under fire from its guns, or from those of the supporting Union gunboat *New Era*. Before making the final assault, Forrest called on the fort to surrender. After some hesitation, and a demand for time to consider the matter, the answer was 'No'. The Confederates then swarmed in without much difficulty. In this encounter, the Northerners suffered 400 casualties in the garrison of 560, half of which were negroes. Union survivors later asserted that the Northerners surrendered as soon as they were first overrun, and were shot down in cold blood by Confederates shouting, 'No quarter! No quarter! Kill the damned niggers! Shoot them down!' This however, has never been proven, and it is doubtful whether Forrest would have ordered, permitted or condoned the massacre of which his men have been accused.

Another outstanding Confederate raider was John Mosby. Like Forrest, he took naturally to soldiering, and soon rose to be adjutant of his regiment, a post which provided frequent scouting assign-

ments, one of which paved the way for Jeb Stuart's famous raid round McClellan's army in the Yorktown Peninsula in June 1862.

When the Confederate Congress passed a Partisan Ranger Act which allowed Rangers to act independently of the army, Mosby began operations on his own account, attacking isolated enemy pickets and detachments and returning with much loot. The Rangers never camped together at night, but each man found his own quarters. They would come together to carry out a raid and then scatter again. For armament they depended mainly on their revolvers. Few carried carbines or sabres, though Mosby himself is usually depicted carrying a sabre. There was no army drudgery, no drill and plenty of loot, so Mosby's Rangers became a popular organization to join.

One night in March 1863 Mosby and his men slipped into the headquarters of General Stoughton. Entering the General's bedroom, Mosby found him sleeping off the effects of a party the night before, with plenty of empty champagne bottles lying about. Mosby woke the General by raising the blankets and disrespectfully slapping him on the behind. Then he bore him off with many of the staff as prisoners.

In the autumn of 1863 Mosby became a sort of Robin Hood in north-west Virginia where the Rangers operated. The Union troops hunted him relentlessly. They never caught him; and he continued his daring raids, hiding in the moun-

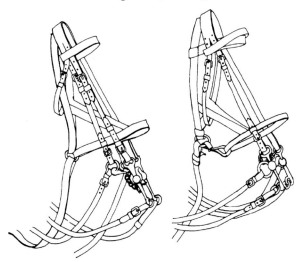

The two principal types of bridles used by the Continental Cavalry. Left, English halter and double bridle; right, a Pelham-style bridle with a bit for use with combined snaffle and curb reins

Federal cavalry scouts entering the depot at Manassas Junction

tains by day and descending on his enemy at night. He was almost as much at home inside the Union lines as within his own, and, with his uniform covered by a poncho, even hobnobbed with enemy soldiers and rode along in their supply columns.

At one period, when Mosby captured some of the young General Custer's messengers, Custer became so enraged that he hanged out of hand some of Mosby's Rangers he had taken. Mosby replied by hanging five of Custer's men in retaliation, and notified Custer's superior, General Sheridan, that this would continue, measure by measure, if this sort of thing went on. It never happened again.

On 13 October 1864 there occurred one of Mosby's most spectacular operations. Beyond Harper's Ferry in Maryland, his Rangers derailed a train and seized $173,000 in currency notes which two paymasters were taking to army headquarters. This particular raid came to be known as the Greenback Raid, and the story of it grew in the telling, so that panic spread among the other paymasters.

Mosby was wounded several times, and rose to

be a colonel before the end of the war. There was some difficulty in his securing the liberal parole terms which Grant had extended to Lee's officers at Appomattox, but this was finally adjusted, and John Mosby returned to the practice of law.

In March 1865 the Union cavalry leader General James H. Wilson made his raid through Alabama, the largest and most successful cavalry raid of the war. Wilson had under him 14,000 well-disciplined and well-armed men whom he had prepared for battle himself. Armed with the Spencer repeating carbine, they were far superior in fire-power to his opponent, General 'Fustest with the Mostest' Forrest's scattered and war-worn troops. Everything had been planned for mobility, and each man had five days' rations, 100 rounds of ammunition and even spare horseshoes. Besides a well-furnished supply train, a light pontoon train of thirty boats was brought along.

Wilson advanced in several separate columns forcing Forrest to weaken his defence by scattering his men over a broad front. These tactics proved completely successful, for, by concentrating quickly when necessary, Wilson was able to overwhelm

17

first one sector of the enemy and then another. On 2 April 1865 he carried the Confederate supply depot at Selma, Alabama, by storm and destroyed its foundries, arsenals and stores. Then he led his mounted men on to Montgomery and did the same there. Receiving news of Lee's surrender at Appomattox Court House, and of President Jefferson Davis's flight towards the south-west, he sent out a force which intercepted and captured the fleeing Confederate President. Altogether General Wilson's well organized march, which was the longest of the war, proved highly successful.

Two other successful Union cavalry commanders were General John Buford and General P. H. Sheridan. Besides Brandy Station, as recorded, Buford distinguished himself on several other occasions. In the Battle of Second Bull Run his was the only formation which vigorously opposed the advance through Thoroughfare Gap of Long-street's Corps when it was coming to the relief of Jackson's Corps, at bay on Stony Ridge. Also, it is said, that without Buford's action, Gettysburg

would not have become one of the decisive battles of history. Lee's army had crossed the Potomac and moved north through the Antietam area into Pennsylvania, and seemed to be threatening Baltimore. At the end of June 1863 it was reported to be at Chambersburg and moving east to seek a store of shoes in the little town of Gettysburg. General Meade gave orders to General Reynolds to move into Gettysburg with the 1 Division and Buford's cavalry. Passing westwards through the town, Buford's men came into contact with the strong Confederate forces advancing towards it, and set to skirmishing with their advanced elements. They then fell back and dismounted, and held McPherson's Ridge until the Iron Brigade came up and reinforced them. By keeping the Confederates out of Gettysburg and gaining valuable time, they enabled Meade to bring his main body into the strong Gettysburg defence position on Culps Hill, Cemetery Hill and Cemetery Ridge, from which they could not be dislodged. Buford thereby played a vital part in the Federal victory at Gettysburg.

General Philip H. Sheridan, and other cavalry generals of the Army of the Potomac, 1864

After graduation from West Point, Phil Sheridan served as an infantry officer on the frontier, and he had risen to the rank of captain at the outbreak of the war. He served as quartermaster for General Halleck in Missouri, and then in May 1862 was appointed colonel of a Michigan volunteer cavalry regiment. After winning distinction for his part in battles in the West, like Chattanooga, he was transferred to command the Cavalry Corps in the east, then about 10,000 men.

The Corps' equipment was by this time good, for the Northern factories were turning out a flood of arms, ammunition and military supplies. The men all had Sharps Carbines, or Spencers. They also had Colt revolvers and, in place of the heavy Prussian sword, a light cavalry sabre which could be fixed to a carbine as a bayonet.

May 1864 was a good month for the Union cavalry. While Grant was pounding Lee in the Wilderness, Sheridan's men moved behind the Confederate army and struck at their communications; and during a brush with Stuart's cavalry at Yellow Tavern, Jeb Stuart was killed, a serious loss to the Southern cause.

Sheridan's next move was to lay waste the Shenandoah Valley. As well as being a natural highway along which the Confederates could advance and outflank Washington, it had become important to the Confederacy for its supplies of grain and farm animals. Sheridan's instructions from Grant were to take all the provisions, forage and stock wanted for his own army, and then destroy the rest, although buildings were best left standing. Sheridan carried out his task most ruthlessly, reporting when he withdrew down the valley that he had destroyed 2,000 barns filled with wheat, hay and farming implements, over seventy mills filled with flour and wheat, and had taken for his army four herds and 3,000 sheep. Sheridan later sent Merritt and his cavalry division to devastate Loudoun County. Here it was reported the following were seized or destroyed: 3,772 horses, 545 mules, 10,918 beef cattle, 12,000 sheep, 15,000 swine, 250 calves, and a great quantity of wheat, oats, tobacco and potatoes. It was during his operation in the Shenandoah that Sheridan's famous ride took place. When the advance down the valley was proceeding steadily,

Sheridan retired to Winchester in the North and left the operations to his subordinates. Then, with General Sheridan twenty miles away, General Jubal Early made a surprise attack on the Union camp at Cedar Creek. A despatch rider was hastily sent north to apprise the General, and found him in bed asleep. Sheridan's reaction on hearing the news was quick. Mounting his best horse, he galloped madly down the valley to take charge of the situation. Meeting stragglers from the field, and then retreating troops, he halted them and ordered them back. When they formed on the side of the road to let him pass, they first cheered him as he dashed down their lines, and then followed him. Solely by the power of his leadership he turned defeat into victory, for the once-beaten Union troops now drove the Confederates from the field. It was not strictly a cavalry battle; but the cavalry completed the defeat of Early's troops and captured large quantities of supplies and arms, and took many hundreds of prisoners; and the battle was won by a great cavalry officer.

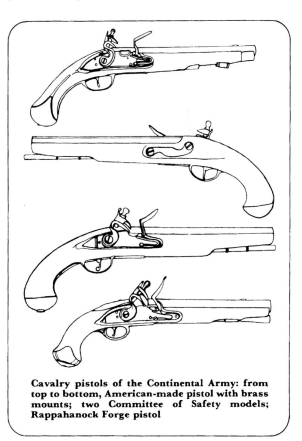

Cavalry pistols of the Continental Army: from top to bottom, American-made pistol with brass mounts; two Committee of Safety models; Rappahanock Forge pistol

The Frontier 1865-90

During and immediately after the Civil War there was considerable unrest on the frontiers, for, being unrestrained, the tribes of the Sioux in the north and the Apaches in the south went on the rampage. In Texas and on the borders of Mexico conditions were almost as bad, for the Comanches as well as the Apaches intensified their frontier raiding, and Mexico itself was in the throes of a civil war between the followers of Napoleon III's protégé, the Emperor Maximilian, and Mexican Liberals led by Señor Juarez. The position became so critical that in May 1865 a strong force under General Sheridan was sent to Texas. The presence of this force, which included two cavalry regiments, encouraged the Mexican Liberals to make fresh efforts so that at last they overcame Maximilian.

The huge volunteer army of the Civil War was in the process of being demobilized; but Congress realized that there was still need for a cavalry force to pacify the Indians on the frontier, so in July 1866 four more regular cavalry regiments were authorized. This made a cavalry force of ten regiments of which the 9th U.S. Cavalry and 10th U.S. Cavalry had negro enlisted men and white officers.

Many operations were carried out against dissident Indians during the period from 1866 to 1890, and two of the most dramatic of these will be described: the battle with Roman Nose's Cheyennes in Colorado, and Custer's last stand against Sioux and North Cheyennes on the Little Bighorn, a tributary of the Yellowstone which itself is a tributary of the Missouri.

In 1866 the Cheyennes under the leadership of Roman Nose were particularly hostile and destructive, constantly raiding isolated settlements, stealing stock and killing settlers. As no regular cavalry was readily available, Major George A. Forsyth of the 9th U.S. Cavalry, with Captain Beecher as second-in-command, was put in charge of fifty frontiersmen who being mostly veterans of the Civil War were well suited to deal with unruly Indians.

In September 1866, well mounted, and armed with seven-shot Spencers and Colts, the column set out. It soon hit the Indians' trail, and from there on followed it along the Republican River into southern Nebraska, reaching a point two hundred miles east of the present-day township of Cheyenne. Here, on the sixth day out, with rations nearly expended, the party encamped. Next morning, a large band of Indians appeared, and Forsyth moved his men down on to an island in the partially dried-up river bed, where he ordered them to dig in. With the horses sadly exposed, and almost acting as ramparts, the party met a long series of Indian charges. It was later estimated that 1,000 Indians were present, and although not all took part in the charges, those who did not formed a circle and kept up a steady fire on the island redoubt from all sides.

The climax came when Roman Nose, a giant of a man in a huge feathered head-dress, charged at the head of his massed warriors. The defenders fired volley after volley without visibly checking the onrush, but when the Indians were almost upon them, Roman Nose fell mortally wounded, and his followers, confused by the death of their leader, retreated. The ring of Indian marksmen remained and kept up a constant fire, and the party had to endure an agonizing siege of nine days living on horseflesh and wild plums. Finally, four men slipped successfully through the ring and summoned help in the form of two troops of the 10th U.S. Cavalry. These quickly galloped to the rescue of the tormented survivors. In the encounter

Colonel Judson Kilpatrick, a classmate of George Armstrong Custer at West Point, was a major-general at 25

content, for in 1868 the Government had allotted them a large agency in the north which included their favourite hunting grounds in the Black Hills country of Wyoming and South Dakota. Then came the discovery of gold in the Black Hills, and the inevitable inroads of covetous whites. The tribes became unsettled. They assembled under the Hunkpapá medicine-man Sitting Bull in the neighbourhood of the Rosebud and Little Bighorn, two tributaries of the Yellowstone River, and began a series of large-scale raids on settlers in the area.

The hostile attitude of Sitting Bull and his followers moved the Commissioner of the Indian Bureau to recommend that force be used to compel the bands to settle down and cease marauding, and in April 1876 General Sheridan was ordered to take the necessary action. Sheridan wanted to carry out an immediate winter campaign to catch the Indians off guard, but the Indian Bureau insisted that they should be given the opportunity to come in, and this caused delay. Sheridan had ordered his department commanders, Brigadier-General George Crook in Omaha, and Brigadier-General Alfred H. Terry in St Paul, to organize some strong columns, and the plan was that three of these, one from Crook's department and two from Terry's, should converge on the place thought to be occupied by the Indians. Although the columns were meant to work in conjunction they were nevertheless made strong enough to defeat on their own the 700 or so Indians the Bureau estimated absent from their agencies. Crook's column was to come up from the south from Fort Fetterman, Gibbon's under Terry was to move in from the west starting from Fort Ellis, and the other column of Terry's was to come from the east from Fort Abraham Lincoln in far-away Dakota.

The eastern column was at first entrusted to Colonel George A. Custer. Custer passed out bottom of his class from West Point at the time of the Civil War. He soon established a reputation as a dashing leader of cavalry, and was made a major-general of Volunteers while still only 25 years old. He commanded a division under Sheridan in the Wilderness and Shenandoah campaigns, and, still under Sheridan, received the white flag of truce sent forward by General

most of the horses were killed, and half the men were either killed or wounded. Beecher, after whom the island was named later, was killed, and Forsyth was severely wounded.

Ten years later, on 25 June 1876, an even more dramatic battle took place. One cause of Indian unrest was the building of the Union Pacific Railway in 1869, which cut through the heart of the buffalo range country. This not only brought settlers, but a horde of commercial buffalo hunters who killed the animals for hides which they sold in the eastern market. The extermination of the buffalo brought an end to the traditional Indian way of life, for they relied on the buffalo for both food and clothing. Among the Indians in the north disturbed by intruders were the tribes of the Sioux and North Cheyennes. For a time they had been

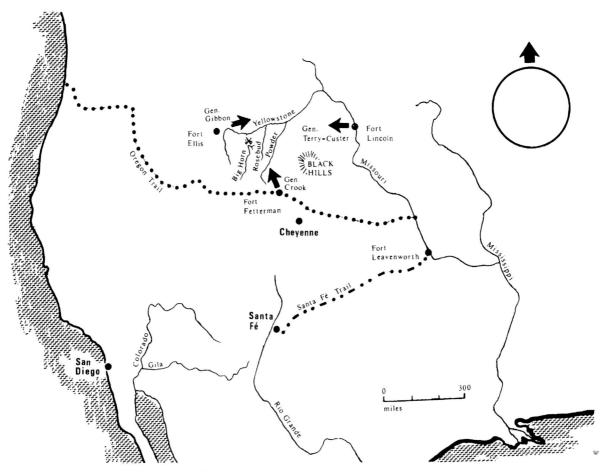

The campaign against the Sioux and Cheyenne, 1876

Lee at Appomattox Court House. Sheridan later gave him the flag as a memento. During the Civil War Custer adopted an extravagant form of dress, and according to eye-witnesses was wearing at Lee's surrender a white sombrero, a flowing scarf, gold sleeves galloons, and his hair as long as a woman's. In the Indian campaigns which followed, however, he apparently had his hair cropped and dressed himself soberly in the brown doeskin of a frontiersman. Before Terry's eastern column got under way, Custer offended President Grant by the nature of the evidence he chose to present at impeachment proceedings against the Secretary of War, and was removed from command. He made frantic efforts for reinstatement, and was eventually allowed to go with the column at the head of his 7th U.S. Cavalry, a regular regiment of renown although there were many recruits in its ranks.

This affair, combined with bad weather, delayed General Terry's two columns, but in early March, in wintry conditions, Crook's 800-strong column got going. In the van leading north from Fort Fetterman was Colonel J. J. Reynolds and six troops[4] of the 3rd U.S. Cavalry. The cavalry came upon an Indian camp by the Powder River. They assaulted it successfully, and drove the bands of Sioux and Cheyennes occupying it away. However, the Indians staged a counter-attack and Reynolds in his turn was thrown back. He rejoined the main column which Crook marched back to Fort Fetterman to refit and try again. The second attempt proved even less successful. On 17 June 1876 Crook's force collided near the source of the Rosebud with 1,000 braves under Crazy Horse, who had been sent south from the main Indian camp to contest the soldiers' advance. After a severe action lasting most of the day, Crook gave the Indians best and once more withdrew to seek reinforcements. The Indians returned to their camp in triumph, but decided nevertheless to move westwards to a more secure situation. They went across from the Rosebud to the Little Bighorn and laid out a new camp-village stretching three miles to the west of the stream. By their victory on the Rosebud the Indians had thrown back one of Sheridan's three columns. Now they were elated and full of confidence.

Terry had by this time set his two columns in motion; but he had not heard of Crook's defeat. Gibbon's western column starting from Fort Ellis moved along the north bank of the Yellowstone. The main body which was mainly infantry did not contact any Indians, but the 2nd U.S. Cavalry ranging south of the river beyond the Rosebud reported their presence in the valley of the Tongue. Terry's two columns were now approaching one another in the neighbourhood of the mouth of the Powder River where Terry set up his headquarters on the *Far West*, a river steamer chartered by the Government to transport supplies for his columns. Receiving the report of Gibbon's scouts concerning enemy presence on the Tongue, Terry sent forward Major Reno with his squadron from the eastern column to carry out a more thorough reconnaissance. Reno's route took him to the Rosebud, and when he turned upstream he discovered the trail left by Crazy Horse's Sioux when returning from their victory over Crook's column. The trail, and other trails of the Indians changing camp, led westwards towards Little Bighorn. Satisfied that the Indian camp-village lay in that direction, Reno retraced his steps to report to General Terry.

On the evening of 21 June 1876 General Terry had a conference with Gibbon and Custer in the cabin of the *Far West* moored to the bank of the Yellowstone near the mouth of the Rosebud. Terry said he estimated the Indian force as 1,000 warriors, and considered that unless they were surrounded and forced into battle they would flee to the western mountains as soon as they discovered the approach of the soldiers. He therefore ordered Gibbon and his foot-soldiers to move back to the mouth of the Bighorn to attack the Indians from the north. Estimating that Gibbon could not be in position before 26 June, he sent Custer and the 7th U.S. Cavalry on a detour round to the south so that by the time they were in position

to attack the camp from that direction, Gibbon would also be ready for a combined assault. Terry fully understood that the more forceful attack would come from Custer's cavalry, and offered him six of Gibbon's Crow scouts, hereditary enemies of the Sioux, to help him on his way. He also offered the squadrons of 2nd U.S. Cavalry with Gibbon's force and two Gatlings (the first machine-guns). Custer gratefully accepted the scouts, but declined the additional cavalry and the Gatlings. The latter he said in truth would slow his march; the 2nd U.S. Cavalry he explained,

The 1st Virginia Cavalry, sketched by Alfred R. Waud whilst a prisoner in their lines

less plausibly, were not necessary as his own men were enough for the task.

On the next morning, Terry gave Custer his orders in writing, saying that he should conform to them unless there was sufficient reason for not doing so. (In the event he did not conform, but whether sufficient reason existed has never been fully decided.) At noon, the 7th U.S. Cavalry with Custer at their head rode past General Terry, and then began their march up the Rosebud. With scouts ahead they advanced steadily and cautiously, and that evening the column went into bivouac by the stream. At 9.00 p.m. the scouts came in and reported that a short distance ahead the Sioux trail discovered by Reno left the Rosebud and led across over the ridge between the stream and the Little Bighorn. Although it was now quite dark Custer ordered an immediate advance, stating that he wanted to reach the summit of the ridge, a distance of ten miles, before daylight. By this action of advancing straight across to the Little Bighorn, and not making a detour to the south as Terry ordered, Custer had now lost all chance of co-operating with Gibbon's column in the north.

In the inky blackness progress was slow; but at 2.00 a.m. they came to the Crow's Nest, a high point on the ridge from which there was a good view in every direction. As soon as it was light, some Indian scouts climbed to its summit from where their sharp eyes were able to pick out immense herds fifteen miles ahead, undoubtedly close to the Sioux camp. Custer, who was by now experienced in this sort of fighting, believed the Indians would strike their camp and escape directly they saw his troops approaching, and that the only way to bring them to battle was to surprise them. He therefore decided to lie in concealment all next day, and then make a surprise night attack. Two circumstances, however, made him change his mind. During the march a pack fell off, and when a sergeant was sent back to recover it he found some Indian warriors examining it. On sighting the sergeant, the Indians rode off, but the Americans' approach had now been revealed. Also, from the top of the Crow's Nest Sioux scouts were noticed at no great distance moving away quickly towards the Indian camp. Because of these two incidents Custer realized that any attempt at surprise was useless. He therefore decided to attack at once.

Custer divided his command into three. He sent Captain Benteen with 125 men on a detour over the bluffs to the south and told him 'to pitch into anything' he might find; he ordered Major Reno to advance with his squadron along the south bank of the tributary running west into Little Bighorn; and he himself advanced at the head of the remainder of the regiment along its north bank. Following opposite banks Custer and Reno advanced cautiously for about nine miles, their lines of march almost parallel, sometimes close together, sometimes as much as 300 yards apart. Shortly after 2.00 p.m. a lone tepee was sighted, and Custer immediately bore down on it. It proved to be the remnant of an Indian village, all the tepees having been removed except for this one which contained the dead body of a warrior.

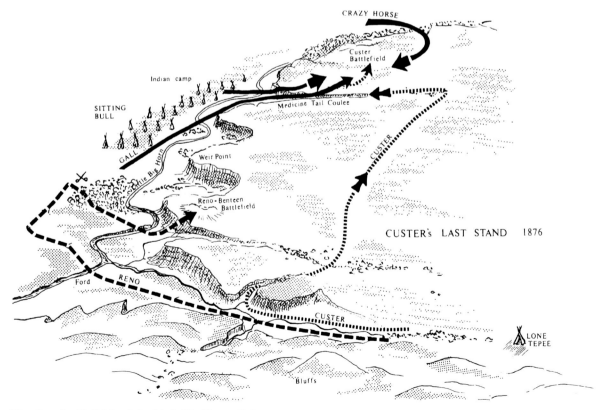

The three battlefields of the Little Big Horn, 1876

Trooper, 1st Continental Light Dragoons, 1778

A

1 Officer, Baylor's Dragoons, 1777
2 Trooper, 3rd Continental Light Dragoons, 1780
3 Officer of Horse, Charles Dabney's Virginia State Legion, 1782–3

B

MICHAEL ROFFE

1 Colonel (Full Dress), 2nd U.S. Light Dragoons, 1812–14
2 Dragoon Sergeant, Colonel Hays's Regiment of Texas Mounted Volunteers, 1847–8
3 Officer, 1st Virginia Volunteer Cavalry, 1861–3

MICHAEL ROFFE

C

Bugler, 3rd U.S. Cavalry, 1865

D

MICHAEL ROFFE

First Sergeant, 6th Pennsylvania Cavalry
(Rush's Lancers), 1863

MICHAEL ROFFE

E

1 Cavalry General, Confederate Army, 1861–5
2 Cavalry Sergeant, Confederate Army, 1862
3 Captain (Full Dress), 5th U.S. Cavalry, 1872

F

1 **Corporal (Campaign Dress), 4th U.S. Cavalry**, 1871
2 **Colonel (Undress), 5th U.S. Cavalry**, 1870
3 **Sergeant Major (Full Dress), 4th U.S. Cavalry**, 1876

MICHAEL ROFFE

G

1 Lieutenant-Colonel, 1st U.S. Volunteer Rough Riders, 1898
2 Trooper, 2nd U.S. Cavalry, 1917
3 Corporal Pathfinder, 1st Cavalry Division (Airmobile), 1967

H

MICHAEL ROFFE

While the scouts were setting it on fire, an interpreter scanning the country ahead noticed a heavy dust cloud a few miles further on, and between it and the tepee a party of Sioux in flight downstream. The man turned in the saddle and shouted, 'There, Colonel, are your Indians! Running like devils!' Instantly Custer ordered the Crow scouts ahead in pursuit, but they refused. Reno was just coming up at the head of his squadron, and Custer sent his adjutant, Cooke, across with a message. It told Reno to go forward as fast as he could, and charge the Indians when he caught them up, adding that he would be supported soon by the whole outfit.

When this order to attack was given, Sitting Bull's camp was not visible. Aside from the small party in flight there were no Indians in sight. The dust indicated a force of some size; but Custer did not realize that 4,000 of the fiercest, bravest and most daring of savages were awaiting Reno in the valley of the Little Bighorn, warriors elated by their victory over Crook's column, and most of them armed with new Winchester repeating rifles.

Reno's squadron, accompanied by Cooke the adjutant, covered the three miles along the tributary (later to be named Reno Creek) to the Little Bighorn at a sharp trot. Sergeant Ryan later wrote, 'We arrived at the bank of the Little Bighorn and waded to the other side, and here there was a very strong current, and there was quicksand about three feet deep. On the other side of the river we made a short halt, dismounted, tightened our saddle girths, and then swung into our saddles.' When the main body reached the far side, the scouts came galloping back to report that the Sioux camp was just ahead, and that the Indian party they were chasing had turned to attack them. Cooke the adjutant now retraced his steps to report to Custer, while Reno drew up his force in the fringe of some trees on the west bank in preparation for the attack. After a few moments spent in forming up Reno led his squadron forward, two troops in line and one in reserve. In this formation they approached the camp, the first few tepees of which could now be seen through the shifting clouds of dust some two miles downstream. Reno called the reserve troop into line with the others, and taking up his position twenty yards in

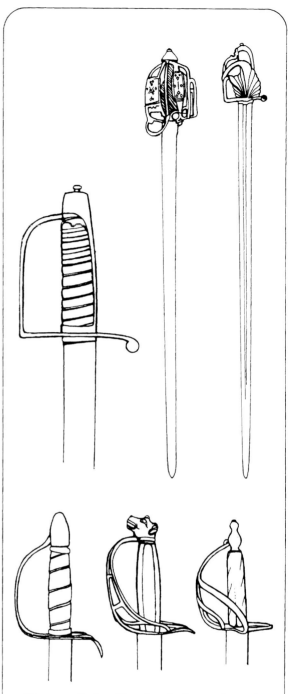

There was little uniformity of sabres and swords among the mounted regiments of Washington's army. Civilian and military models, village-made models by the local smithy, family heirlooms, and imported and captured blades – all were used. The selection illustrated shows: American stirrup-hilted sabre; other sabre hilts including one with a dog's-head pommel; two broadswords, one basket-hilted, the other a French model

front gave the order for 'The Charge' to be sounded. Then he led his men forward at the gallop. A heavily timbered bend of the river jutted into the valley on the squadron's right, beyond which flowed the rippling river, and to the front between them and the nearest tepees of the camp a quarter of a mile away were hundreds of yelling Indians. Some of these were already starting to ride round Reno's squadron's left flank, and many were already starting to shoot at the cavalrymen.

Reno was somewhat at a loss as he started forward into battle. Looking back he saw no sign of anyone coming to his support, and by now he had expected the aid of Custer's men, and perhaps of Benteen's squadron as well. Noticing the huge numbers of his opponents, and not wishing to sacrifice his command by leading them straight into the jaws of death, he speedily made a change of plan. Instead of continuing towards the camp, he led his men across into the trees on their right, and having ordered them to dismount, got them to take up a defensive position and send their horses back among the trees for protection. For something like half an hour there followed a battle in the wood, all the while the Indians moving round the troopers' left flank. At that stage Reno had lost only one man shot through the breast, but his ammunition was running low, and a quick

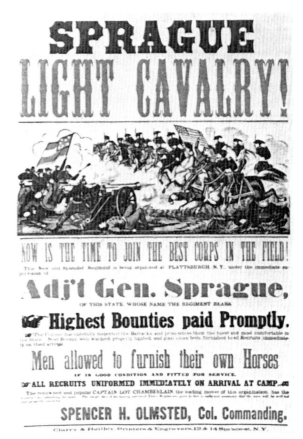

A seductive recruiting poster. The picture is honest about the type of enemy to be faced, but perhaps less so about the effect of heavy guns on a cavalry charge

A sketch by Winslow Homer of the 6th Pennsylvania Lancers during the Peninsular Campaign

survey of the situation convinced him that he must get out. He gave the order to mount, and lined up his men in a clearing in the trees. Then, already beset by Indians who had rushed into the wood after them, they formed an irregular column and galloped out, pistols drawn, in a dash for the ford they had crossed earlier. Troopers and scouts were now falling: some died in the wood, others

were killed as they emerged; and the pressure of the masses of Indians blocking the escape route was too strong for the reduced force to break through. Realizing this, Reno swerved to the left and led his men towards a place on the river bank more than a mile downstream from where they had first crossed. The head of the column reached the river in fair order, for only a few Indians were encountered on the left; but on the right were hundreds who raced along beside them, pumping their new Winchesters as fast as they could load and fire, and ducking behind the shoulders of their ponies whenever a trooper raised a pistol. At the river-bank a drop of six feet to the water below checked the horses, many of which refused to jump. The pressure of those behind forced them over the crumbling bank, and down they went, men and horses floundering together in the water. Meanwhile, the pursuing Indians poured a steady rain of bullets into the jammed troops so that 29 out of 112 who reached the river were killed and scalped before the crossing was negotiated. On the far bank the land rose to a hill towering above the stream, and up its slope the panting men and horses struggled. As they arrived, the discomfited scattered remnants of the three troops were gathered together and reformed on the hill's flat summit. The uninjured were then hastily posted to fend off the next Sioux attack. Had many Indians followed across the river Reno's squadron might well have been wiped out. Those Indians, however, who did cross and were advancing up the slopes, had their attention diverted along with the rest of the warriors from the camp to another part of the field where four miles to the north Custer's squadron was advancing on them.

Meanwhile, Benteen's detachment, which had been diverted from the route the regiment followed, had travelled towards the bluffs to the south and found no evidence of the presence of Indians there. The ground was cut with innumerable gullies and ravines and consisted of bad lands of a rugged type not easily passable by anything but goats. After going about twelve miles, Benteen felt satisfied that nothing was to be found, and turned back in the direction in which the regiment had been heading when he left it. After covering fifteen more miles, he reached their line of march near the burnt-out remains of the tepee which had contained the dead warrior. Continuing to follow Custer's trail, he encountered first a sergeant sent back to hurry up the ammunition, and then an orderly with a message telling him there was a big Indian camp ahead, and that Custer wanted him to hurry, and bring with him the pack animals

with the spare ammunition three miles farther along the trail. Benteen's detachment came to a rise in the ground, and on mounting it saw the Valley of Little Bighorn before them. There in the dust and smoke things were happening which must at the time have dismayed them. An overwhelming force of yelling, painted Sioux, sweeping and swooping from all directions, were riding down and killing the rear members of a little band of soldiers who were trying to reach the river and the safety of Reno's defence position on the hill on the other side. It was the last of his command who had been unhorsed and left behind in the mad rush from the wood.

Some of the Indians halted and opened fire from across the river upon Benteen's men as they appeared on the skyline, but the range was too great and the shots fell harmlessly at their feet. Drawing pistols, Benteen's men trotted forward towards Reno's improvised defensive position on the hilltop. As they came up, Reno with his head tied with a handkerchief ran forward to meet them exclaiming, 'For God's sake, Benteen, halt your command and help me, for I have lost half my men.'

Many of Reno's party, including Reno, were obviously overwrought. Some were firing their revolvers aimlessly at Indians out of range thousands of yards away. A subaltern of K Troop, however, seemed cool enough. 'I'm damned glad to see you, Benteen,' he said. 'We had a big fight in the valley and got whipped like hell.' With the arrival of Benteen, it was he who really took command. Benteen was a man of great presence and as brave as a lion. He quickly

The 2nd Cavalry in the 1870s, wearing full dress

Two impressions of Custer's last battle against the hordes of Sitting Bull on 25 June 1876

brought order out of confusion. He divided his party's ammunition with Reno's men who had almost exhausted theirs in the fight in the valley; he sent off a messenger to hurry up the ammunition-mules; and he set about reconstituting the defences around the top of the hill.

For a time, however, they were not menaced by the Indians, the greater part of whom had left to join in the fight in the north, the battle noises of which Reno's and Benteen's men could now hear distinctly. As a series of distant volleys rang out clearer than before, Captain Weir of D Troop sprang to his feet and exclaimed, 'If that's Custer, we ought to go and help him.' He then asked Reno's permission for his unit to go to Custer's aid. When Reno demurred, he rode forward with his troop without receiving it.

Later, Reno changed his mind and followed Weir with the whole of his command. Well in advance, Weir was the first to top the pinnacle (later called Weir Point) on the ridge, and from it he saw in the distance three miles away the smoke and dust of a battle. He was just ordering his men to advance towards it when hundreds of Indian warriors rode up the slope towards them and

drove them back. Soon the whole of Reno's command was in retreat. They were forced back to their old defence position on the hilltop, and there hemmed in by a ring of Indian braves. For three hours, until the light began to fail, the 350 troopers fought back against the Indians pressing in on them from all sides. Relief came with darkness when, their blood-lust seemingly satisfied for the moment, the Indians returned across the river to their camp for a great war dance illuminated by bonfires.

When darkness set in the defenders of the hilltop improved their defences. Sergeant Ryan wrote: 'We went to work with what tools we had, consisting of two spades, our knives and tin cups, and, in fact, we used pieces of hard tack boxes for spades, and commenced throwing up temporary works. We also formed breastworks from boxes of hard bread, sacks of bacon, sacks of corn and oats, blankets, and in fact anything that we could get hold of. During the night ammunition and rations reached us.'

At dawn a single rifle shot rang out followed at a short interval by another. It was the enemy's signal to renew the attack, and soon from all

directions came the crashing fire of the Sioux. During the fiercest of the fighting, bugle calls were heard and the hills were scanned for the signs of a relief column. But it was found to be a captured bugle blown by the Sioux as a ruse.

The Indians worked themselves ever closer taking every advantage of terrain and sage bush to escape being hit. Massing first in the south, they hurled themselves at Benteen's part of the line. Believing the best means of defence was to attack, Benteen called his men to their feet and led them in a counter-charge against the Indians which threw them back in confusion. Next Benteen went across to Reno's part of the perimeter and persuaded him to carry out a similar manoeuvre, which achieved equal success.

Thirst became a torment for the defenders, especially among the wounded in the improvised hospital housed in a shallow depression in the centre of the position; but volunteers gallantly slipped down to the river and filled canteens which they brought back to afford some relief. For this feat nineteen men later received the Congressional Medal of Honour. Early in the afternoon the siege relaxed, and by late afternoon only an occasional shot reminded the defenders to stay under cover. The Indians then fired the prairie grass around their camp village, and a thick wall of smoke hid their tepees from view. Soon, an immense procession of horsemen, women and children on foot, and loose ponies and dogs emerged from behind the smoke. The Indians were departing. The ordeal of Reno's and Benteen's men was over.

The Oglala Sioux Chief Low Dog, and the Hunkpapá Chief Gall both took part in the battles against the 7th U.S. Cavalry. From their accounts later, it seems that Custer, not realizing the vast numbers in the village, thought that the Indians would escape him if he did not attack immediately. Therefore after following Reno's trail for a mile or two, he turned north well short of the ford by which Reno's men crossed the Little Bighorn. No doubt he had originally intended to reinforce Reno's attack; but on second thoughts he decided to move round to the north and come in on the village from that direction at the same time that Reno's squadron was attacking it from the south. It is known that soon after turning off north Custer sent back a sergeant to hurry up the reserve ammunition, and later an orderly to bring Benteen's squadron to his support – not to support Reno, it should be noted, which is what actually occurred.

Up to the northern battlefield Custer seems first to have led his men down the ravine named Medicine Tail Coulee, with the intention of crossing the river and attacking the camp. In this he was thwarted by a vast horde of charging Indians who forced him up again on to the top of the escarpment which flanks the river on the east. Afterwards, on his improvised defence position on the summit, he was attacked by vast bands of Indians moving in on him from all directions.

According to Chief Gall, Sitting Bull did not lead his men in the battle. He remained in his tepee making medicine to propitiate the supernatural. The principal leaders were Gall who, after attacking Reno's squadron, charged up at the head of his warriors from the south, and Crazy Horse, General Crook's conqueror, who led his men right round the north of Custer's position and swept in at the rear. Other Indian hordes crossed the river due west of Custer's position, pressed up Deep Coulée, and crashed into his flank.

Caught in rough terrain unsuited to mounted action, and surrounded by overwhelming numbers of Sioux and Cheyenne warriors, Custer's squadron swiftly disintegrated. The troops (companies) seem to have made individual stands fighting on foot against waves of Indians that surged in from every direction. One troop covered the south of Custer's selected battleground, another the east, while on the west two more which had slipped down into a ravine were crushed by sheer weight of numbers. Yet another troop straddled the central ridge, and at the north end, where Crazy Horse's men blocked an escape route, a knot of fifty gathered around Custer and his red and blue personal pennant, shot their horses for breastworks, and fought to the last round and the last man. Inspired by their most gallant leader, they fought on for hours; but by 5.00 p.m. the only living member of Custer's command on the whole of the northern battlefield was an officer's horse, Comanche. Badly wounded this creature limped its way to safety. It was the sole survivor of Custer's last stand.

General Miles and other cavalry officers viewing a hostile Indian camp near Pine Ridge, Dakota, in 1891

An 1891 print showing the field dress of various arms. Centre, a field officer; left and right, Indian scout and cavalry corporal; extreme left and right, horse artillery and infantry

On Reno's hill during the late afternoon the men watched the Indians depart with relief tinged with a fear that they might return. During the following night the troopers buried their dead, still fearful that dawn might see the renewal of the attack. At daybreak, however, when they looked out down the valley, they saw a comforting long blue column marching towards them. It was General Terry and the 2nd U.S. Cavalry.

When the relief party arrived, they reported the sad fate of Custer's squadron whose bodies a scouting party had discovered on the hill in the north. Most of them had been stripped, scalped and mutilated, but, strangely, Custer's body had been left untouched. There he lay, they said, like a Saxon hero surrounded by the bodies of his men-at-arms. His expression was so peaceful that it seemed he had fallen asleep rather than met his death in the heat of battle.

After Little Bighorn, the great Sioux and Cheyenne hordes broke up and went their separate ways, pursued by reconstituted columns under General Terry and General Crook. By autumn many of the Indians slipped back to their agencies to surrender. Next spring, Crazy Horse gave in. Sitting Bull took part of his people over the border into Canada. He vowed he would never accept the restrictions of a reservation. Finally, however, disappointed in the food supplies available in Canada, he too surrendered. Thus, the campaigns carried out by the United States Cavalry during 1876–77 accomplished their objectives. The Indians were compelled to abandon the unceded hunting grounds and accept Government control in their allotted reservations; and what was more, the frightened Chiefs were forced to sell the mineral-bearing Black Hills.

From Horses
to Helicopters

The period after the pacification of the frontier at the end of the nineteenth century up to the beginning of the First World War was one in which U.S. regular cavalry regiments had few opportunities to distinguish themselves. There did occur, however, in 1898, the storming of San Juan Hill at Santiago, Cuba, by the 1st U.S. Cavalry, the coloured 9th Cavalry and the Rough Riders; also operations in the Philippines were carried out by the 4th U.S. Cavalry and other regiments; and General Pershing led a chase of the anti-American faction leader Pancho Villa in Mexico in 1916. In the last operation, seven regular cavalry regiments were involved, and Captain George S. Patton of the 8th U.S. Cavalry distinguished himself.

The Rough Riders had the official name of the 1st United States Volunteer Cavalry, and were mostly recruited from Arizona, New Mexico, Oklahoma and Indian Territory. The men were largely cowboys or prospectors who were used to horses and life in the open. They were mixed with a small number of Eastern college men who were sneered at as dudes, but secretly much admired. They were commanded by Colonel Teddy Roosevelt, later to become President of the United States.

The landing took place near Santiago on the south coast of Cuba, and the regiments joined the division of the old Confederate cavalryman General Wheeler. Although horses were landed, the jungle proved too dense for many to be used, and the cavalry had to storm on foot the strongly fortified position defending Santiago, called San Juan Hill. Colonel Roosevelt was on horseback when he started to lead his men up the hill, but was stopped near the summit by a wire fence, and had to continue on foot like the rest. A spirited assault carried out by a combined force of the 1st U.S. Cavalry, the coloured 9th Cavalry and the Rough Riders won the hill; but only after a tough fight on the summit in which there were 375 casualties out of the 2,300 cavalrymen engaged. However, the carrying of the earthworks of San Juan Hill, defended by Spanish infantry armed with modern Mausers, may be claimed as a very creditable cavalry victory.

In 1899 there was trouble in the Philippines when Filipino insurgents who had been fighting the Spaniards turned upon American troops when it became clear that these were there to stay. General Wheeler on his return from Cuba was sent to the Philippines to restore order, and for his task of apprehending the troublemakers was assigned the eight available regular cavalry regiments and the 11th U.S. Volunteer Cavalry. It was primarily a junior officers' war, with constant fighting and skirmishing in jungle and back country. Among those who gained distinction was Captain John J. Pershing, of whom much was

Lieutenant-colonel Theodore Roosevelt in the uniform of the 1st U.S. Volunteer Cavalry ('Teddy's Terrors') in 1898

to be heard later. It was not until March 1901 that the principal insurgent leader Aguinaldo was captured, but after that the war was virtually over.

When, in 1910, President Diaz, who had controlled the country with an iron hand, abdicated, Mexico was torn with revolutions. Internecine fighting between Mexican factions threatened

Pershing crosses the Rio Grande after the Mexican bandit Pancho Villa, 1916

American lives and property, and the worst of the marauders was the anti-American Pancho Villa. In 1916, after years of unrest, Villa raided the border town of Columbus, New Mexico, where the 13th U.S. Cavalry were stationed. Their sentries were on the alert in the camp on the south side of the town, and quickly called the Regiment to arms. The encounter with Villa's men took place in the main street of the town, where Mexicans had set fire to the hotel. This proved their undoing, for the light from the blaze showed them up as easy targets for the troopers, and a deadly fusillade drove them off leaving sixty-seven of their number dead for a loss of seven Americans.

The raid on Columbus led to the organization of a powerful American punitive expedition under the command of Brigadier-General John J. Pershing. This he conducted with the same skill he had shown in routing the insurgents in the Philippines while a junior officer. But the Mexican

administration, which should have assisted, proved a great hindrance to the American columns. It refused them permission to use the railroads and telegraph lines, and even forbade them to march through the towns.

The main body of the expedition, which consisted of seven regular cavalry regiments, set up headquarters south of the border in the Mexican state of Chihuahua, and then sent out several cavalry columns to trail Pancho Villa and bring him in dead or alive. They never managed to do so; but they fought several engagements with rebel bands, defeated and dispersed them, and killed a number of Villa's most able lieutenants. One exploit involved Lieutenant George S. Patton of the 8th U.S. Cavalry. Patton was out buying forage with seven companions when he came upon a large ranch-house belonging to a leader of a Villa band. Suspecting that the owner might well be at home, although there was no sign of him, Patton posted his men all round the ranch before attempting to enter. His hunch proved correct, for three horsemen armed with rifles and pistols suddenly emerged at a gallop. Patton had orders not to fire unless identity was certain, but directly the *Villistas* opened fire, he drew his pistol and killed all three. This gave Patton such a liking for 'pistol-packing' that from then on he always carried in his belt a pair of pearl-handled pistols.

The two great wars which followed gave little or no opportunity for the employment of horsed cavalry. In the First World War only the 2nd U.S. Cavalry went overseas, and they were given the uncongenial task of running remount depots. The only noteworthy action was when Captain E. N. Harmon of the 2nd U.S. Cavalry led a makeshift squadron in pursuit of the retreating Germans at the very end of the war in 1918. The squadron captured a number of prisoners including a staff officer riding a fine black horse, and Captain Harmon seized the animal and rode it for the rest of the campaign. There was one further distinction, of course, for the cavalry in the First World War. It was the old cavalryman General John J. Pershing who was chosen to command the American Expeditionary Force in France.

When World War II began, the Philippines Scouts, or 26th U.S. Cavalry, were still mounted.

A cavalry trooper photographed in France in 1917

Troopers of the 13th Cavalry loading packhorses with ·30 calibre machine-gun and ammunition

Cavalry training in 1923

Under Colonel Clinton Pierce, with American and Philippine officers and Philippine troopers, they resisted gallantly the Japanese assaults on Luzon and Bataan, and are said to have been responsible for enabling General Wainwright to get away safely from the Philippines.

In 1942 the 1st Cavalry Division was dismounted and trained for warfare in the jungle on the islands of the Pacific. They fought with great distinction and were the first to return to Manila, following which they received warm praise from General MacArthur for the manner in which they had conducted themselves.

Several cavalry officers were chosen to command armoured divisions in World War II, among them E. N. Harmon of World War I fame. His 2nd Armoured Division did so well in combat that it came to be known as the 'Hell on Wheels' division.

One of the most successful commanders in World War II was George S. Patton, who had learnt his trade with the 8th U.S. Cavalry. The thrust and drive he displayed leading his troops out of the Cotentin peninsula through St Lo, to sweep not only south and west into Britanny but also eastwards towards Paris, had all the hallmarks of a cavalry trained leader. It was quite in the tradition of Captain May and Colonel Custer.

Immediately after the war a United States Constabulary was formed which was classed as Cavalry and whose men wore yellow Cavalry scarves; but in 1948 all the Cavalry was officially absorbed into the armoured arm, and a tank was superimposed on the crossed sabres of the Cavalry insignia. The name Cavalry, however, was retained, and several units so named have won distinction in recent times.

At 4.00 a.m. on Sunday 25 June 1950 a North Korean army smashed through the flimsy defences along the 38th parallel and poured into South Korea, crossing a frontier which had only political and ideological significance, being the boundary drawn up between the Russian troops in the north and the American troops in the south after they had entered Korea at the very end of World War II in 1945.

By chance, in June 1950, the Russians were boycotting the Security Council of the United

Nations, so at the emergency meeting following the invasion the Secretary-General was able to get a majority of the nations to support a resolution to order North Korea to withdraw its armed forces, and later to pass a recommendation that 'all member nations should actively help South Korea to repel the North Koreans and restore international security'. Some twenty member nations responded and sent either military forces or medical units; but only the United States, and to a much less degree the British Commonwealth, made significant contributions.

A helicopter of the 1st Cavalry

The North Koreans with Russian-built tanks were more than a match for the ill-equipped Republic of South Korea (ROK) forces. Pouring over the border, they captured Seoul, the capital, and rolled on south towards the port of Pusan in the south-east corner of the peninsula.

The United States had four divisions in Japan, including the 1st Cavalry Division under General Hobart R. Gay, and these were despatched to stiffen South Korean resistance. With the help of the United States 5th Air Force they managed to establish a large defensive area around Pusan. After which, General MacArthur staged a dual offensive. An amphibious landing was made at Inchon on the west coast, and at the same time a force from the Pusan perimeter attacked northwards. In the van of the Pusan force were the men of the 1st Cavalry Division, and they were the first to link up with the troops landed at Inchon.

Having cleared South Korea, General MacArthur was given permission to invade North Korea and establish law and order there. The advance north was made in three great prongs with the addition of an amphibious landing, this time at Wonsan on the north-east coast. The 1st Cavalry Division advanced with the western prong up to Unsan, seventy-five miles from the Yalu River and the border of China.

At this stage in October 1950, just when the war was believed won, the Chinese entered the conflict. Thirty divisions of Chinese volunteers, supported by MiGs piloted by Chinese, crossed the Yalu.

On the night of 31 October hostile troops surrounded the 8th U.S. Cavalry Regiment at Unsan. ROK infantry held the east side, but the Cavalry faced the Chinese in every other quarter.

A withdrawal was decided on, and the 3rd Battalion of the 8th Cavalry was given the task of guarding the bridge over the Nammyon River, north-west of Unsan, until orders for withdrawal were received. About 3.00 a.m. when only the outlying picquets were on the alert, a small column of men approached the bridge, and were taken for ROKs and allowed to pass. Suddenly they and other Chinese who had followed charged into the headquarters area, shooting, bayoneting and tossing satchel charges or grenades into the standing vehicles. Awakened by the din the men of the 3rd Battalion crawled out of their foxholes, where they had gone to sleep while awaiting the signal for withdrawal, and went into action. In Cowboy-and-Indian style they fought all over the area, crouching behind jeeps to fire at the enemy. Finally, when mortar fire began to fall among them, some fought their way out into the dark hills to the south in twos and threes and tried to reach friendly lines.

Many, however, stayed behind under the Battalion commander Major Robert J. Ormond. Efforts to break through and rescue these men made by the 5th U.S. Cavalry failed, but some men of the 2nd Battalion of the 8th Cavalry who had been hiding in the hills, broke through and joined the 3rd Battalion remnants.

Early on the morning of 4 November, all the augmented group of survivors decided to try to escape to the southern hills. Leaving the wounded under the battalion surgeon to surrender to the Chinese, they made off in small groups through drenching rain towards Ipsok and safety; but short of the American lines they were surrounded again by Chinese and the whole process had to be repeated. Only a few of this force eventually reached safety. Some who were taken prisoner escaped to rejoin the regiment days later; others were captured, and several of the badly wounded, including Major Ormond, died in captivity and were buried by the Chinese, who to the Americans' surprise treated their captives much more humanely than the North Koreans had done.

Altogether, the 8th Cavalry lost more than half its authorized strength at Unsan, and a great share of its equipment; but its men had fought there in accordance with the great traditions of the Cavalry arm.

After the distinguished service of the 1st Cavalry Division in the Korean war, and several years spent guarding the Truce Line in Korea, its colours were returned to Fort Benning, Georgia, and the division's name changed to 1st Cavalry Division (Air Mobile).

In the new role as soldiers of the sky the men of the 1st Cavalry Division were soon fighting again, this time in Vietnam, where although their horses have gone – and even their armoured vehicles – the spirit of the Dragoons and of the Mounted Rifles and of the Cavalry is still found. On 1 January 1966 near An Khe in South Vietnam, the Division despatched its psychological warfare plane over the Viet Cong lines with its loudspeaker blaring out the message: 'This is the Year of the Horse [Oriental calendar], and we are the horsemen come to seek you out and destroy you.'

NOTES

1. The Texas Rangers entered a fight uttering horrible shrieks and are said to have been the originators of the 'Rebel Yell' used by Jackson's troops in the Civil War to frighten their opponents.

2. Robert E. Lee passed out of West Point into the Engineers. Later he was Lieutenant-Colonel of the 2nd Cavalry and in the Civil War was Commander-in-Chief of the Confederate forces in the East.

3. General McClellan, who led the Union forces in the Peninsular and Antietam campaigns had served in the 1st Cavalry and been a member of a commission of American officers which toured Europe and visited the scene of the Crimean War. From this trip McClellan brought back the saddle used by the Prussians, formed on a Hungarian saddle tree, and this model, with certain modifications, was adopted by the U.S. Army for its mounted troops. The 'McClellan Saddle' remained standard equipment until the horse cavalry was abolished in 1942.

4. At this time a cavalry troop was usually called a company, and a cavalry squadron was a battalion.

The Plates

A Trooper, 1st Continental Light Dragoons, 1778

Cavalry Uniform in the early years of the revolution was always in a state of catching up with events, for dress regulations were published in the knowledge that materials were not often available, and both officers and men continued to wear civilian clothes or the uniforms of their former companies, which differed widely from each other. The first unit of cavalry was formed during 1776; by December 'a coat, a cap, a pair of leather breeches and a pair of boots and spurs' was the provision at public expense. It was not until 1778 that the regulation uniform became widespread; brown coats with green lapels, cuffs and collars,

green waistcoats, leather breeches, gilt or yellow buttons of regimental pattern, and black leather caps with green turbans and yellow tassels. This trooper is a reasonably well-dressed man of the time, though his coat has tails and his headgear is fanciful.

B1 Officer, Baylor's Dragoons, 1777

In January 1777 Colonel George Baylor was authorized to raise a regiment of horse, and for some time it was inevitably known as Baylor's Dragoons rather than its more formal title of The Third Continental Regiment of Light Dragoons. Knowledge of the uniform is scanty, except that the rifle-shirt is well-known and examples have survived. The body was made of a single piece of linen, an opening out for the neck and the front, and the cape stitched on. The buttons were of bone or cloth-covered wood. Fringes were made by cutting strips of linen and pulling out the threads on both edges. Note the obsolete abbreviation of 'United States' on the wooden canteen.

B2 Trooper, 3rd Continental Light Dragoons, 1780

The uniform for the early days of the revolution is hardly known, but after May 1779 the jackets were white and lined and faced with blue. A double-breasted waistcoat, leather belt and silver epaulettes and buttons were also worn, but how widely is not known; white was a more likely colour for the waistcoat than the blue depicted

A standard of the 2nd Continental Dragoons bearing the motto PAT^t CONCITA FULM NATI; centre, a second colour of the same regiment bearing another version of the motto, PAT^A CONCITA FULM^{NT} NATI; right, the Eutaw standard of the 3rd Continental Dragoons late in the Revolutionary War, traditionally supposed to have been cut from a damask curtain

here, though colours still varied considerably. The dress here represents a period of change when the regiment was joining the Southern Army in 1780 and green facing cloth was being issued. One authority, followed here, gives 'a black jockey cap with foxtail and red turban' as the headgear. The cartridge box depicted is of dark brown leather with twelve tin pipes for the cartridges. The weapon is a French carbine.

B3 Officer of Horse, Charles Dabney's Virginia State Legion, 1782–3

The Legion was comprised of remnants of the 3rd State Regiment, Major Nelson's Corps of Cavalry, Captain John Rogers's dismounted Illinois dragoons, and Captain Christopher Roan's artillery; and at first the men wore the clothing of their former units. The first State issue of clothing was cloth for the coats, which were blue with facings of the same colour, lined with white serge. The addition of red facings could be afforded only by a few officers, of whom this man is one. He wears also a white, long-sleeved waistcoat, leather boots and breeches, and a brown cloth cloak lined with white corduroy. Equipment carried on the horse included deerskin holsters, mail pillions, carbine, and sword.

C1 Colonel, Full Dress, 2nd U.S. Light Dragoons, 1812–14

The two remaining troops of cavalry in the U.S. forces were enlarged into two regiments for the second war against the British, 1812–15. This colonel is dressed in dark grey jacket and breeches

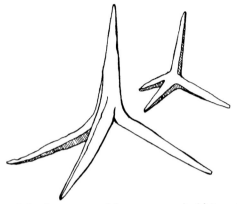

One of the longest-surviving weapons in history is the caltrops, a four-pointed piece of iron scattered by the thousand on the ground to impede the progress of cavalry. Whichever way they fall, there is always one sharp point sticking up vertically. They were used in the Revolution, largely by the British

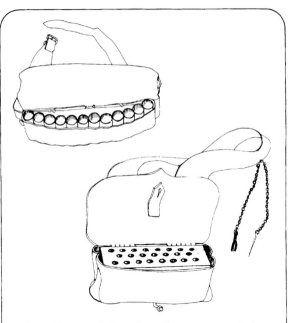

Cartridges, and also often flints, were carried in a cartridge box, usually a leather bag with a large flap (and sometimes a smaller flap beneath) to keep out the rain, containing a wooden block with twenty-four holes to hold the cartridges. A special type for the use of cavalry had twelve tin pipes to hold the cartridges. Cavalry wore their boxes buckled around the waist in front – see colour plate B2

with silver lace, and a crimson sash like the British officers of the period. The cavalry pattern sabre hung from a white or buff waistbelt on a buff sling and sported a silver swordknot. The high collar and the cut of the jacket are similar to the British light dragoons of the period. The helmet is of black japanned leather with white metal mountings resembling the French Napoleonic-period dragoon helmet. The horsetail was common to all ranks, as was the plume, though non-combatant officers such as quartermasters had green plumes.

C2 Dragoon Sergeant, Col. Hays's Regiment of Texas Mounted Volunteers, 1847–8

The Texas Mounted Volunteers were raised to subdue Mexican guerrilla activity after Major General Winfield Scott's capture of Mexico City, and few if any of them had conventional uniforms. The man shown here is attached to the regiment as an instructor in the use of the captured Mexican sabres with which the volunteers were equipped after a fight near Matamoros; such a sabre is the one he wears slung from his belt.

C3 Officer, 1st Virginia Volunteer Cavalry, 1861–3
This superior volunteer regiment was composed of several mounted companies from the Valley of Virginia, including the Rockbridge Dragoons, Amelia Light Dragoons, and Washington Mounted Rifles, and commanded by the famous 'Jeb' Stuart. Many of the men had considerable wealth and social standing and their horses and equipment were of the finest. The uniform depicted was worn by all officers at the beginning of the war. The collar star represents the rank of major; the yellow facings indicate the cavalry branch.

D Bugler, 3rd U.S. Cavalry, 1865
In the first year of the Civil War all mounted units of the Union Army – cavalry, dragoons, and mounted riflemen – were reorganized and re-numbered in Cavalry Divisions. The Mounted Riflemen became the 3rd Cavalry. The saddle shown is the McClellan Saddle introduced by General McClellan, after some modifications, from the type used by the Prussians. It remained standard equipment until 1942.

E First Sergeant, 6th Pennsylvania Cavalry (Rush's Lancers), 1863
The only lancer unit in the Civil War, the 6th Pennsylvania wore standard U.S. Cavalry uniform apart from the lance itself. The single button and braid on the collar was a feature of several units raised from volunteers as opposed to expanded from pre-war regulars. Enlisted men wore brass crossed sabres on the crown of the kepi. Brass shoulder scales were worn earlier but by 1863 had been discontinued. All leather is black, including the boots worn under the trousers. Gauntlets were optional. The lance was not a success, and was more a hindrance than an effective weapon when the regiment was forced to chase around the countryside after the elusive Jeb Stuart. Nine feet in length, with an eleven-inch, three-edged point, it had a counter-weight at the bottom, a scarlet swallow-tail pennon, and a black leather sling for when the lance was carried at rest. In February 1863 twelve men in each company were issued with Sharps carbines, and later the lance was replaced with this excellent weapon throughout the regiment. The 6th fought dismounted at Gettysburg and made good use of their new car-

bines. The light cavalry pattern sabre with which they were issued was another disappointment; defective in temper, it proved most unreliable.

F1 Cavalry General, Confederate Army, 1861–5
He is wearing his double-breasted full dress coat with the lapels buttoned back. The fringed waist sash, trouser seam stripe, cuffs and collar, are all of cavalry yellow. A kepi would be more correct, but most officers preferred the more flamboyant hat, and according to their fancy would decorate it with ostrich feathers.

F2 Cavalry Sergeant, Confederate Army, 1862
The enlisted man's grey uniform with gilt buttons and yellow facings, as seen in all Civil War films, this should be regarded as parade-ground order. The date is carefully chosen – not so early in the war that regulation supplies would not have caught up with demand, but very soon after! Many soldiers ended the war dressed much as they had begun it, except for the addition of captured Union weapons and boots.

F3 Captain, Full Dress, 5th U.S. Cavalry, 1872
With the Civil War ended, attention was promptly switched to subduing the Plains Indians, and from 1871–4 the regiment was stationed in Arizona, fighting the Apaches. This captain's full dress uniform includes the black felt helmet with horse-hair plume, gold cords and tassels, and gilt trimmings. The gold cord shoulder knots of Russian pattern have just been introduced. The two gold lace stripes on the cuff designate his rank as a company officer below the rank of major.

G1 Corporal, Campaign Dress, 4th U.S. Cavalry, 1871
Here is the hero of a hundred Wild West films – the cavalryman who fought in the Indian Wars. In 1871 the 4th Cavalry were operating in West Texas, New Mexico and Oklahoma against the Apaches. The most noticeable feature of the uniform is the black hat, notoriously badly designed for it lost its shape at the first rainstorm, and could often be kept on only by tying the brim up into a cocked-hat effect. The bandana is an individual purchase; all troopers wore them, under or over the jacket. The jacket illustrated is one of several styles, an issue garment cut down from a frock-coat with the collar worn rolled open. The Sharps or

Spencer carbine was carried slung on a shoulder belt, not in a saddle bucket.

G2 Colonel, Undress, 5th U.S. Cavalry, 1870

He wears the regulation forage cap with leather chin-strap and embroidered crossed sabres. The herring-bone loops of the jacket are formed of $\frac{1}{4}$ inch braid, the coat and collar edging of $\frac{1}{2}$ inch braid. The trousers are of the same light blue colour as for enlisted men (see plate G1), with the same $1\frac{1}{2}$-inch yellow stripe. His belt shows the brass eagle plate used since the Civil War and not to be replaced until, officially, 1872 and, in practice, 1874–5, by the oval 'U.S.' plate. The holster and pistol cap pouch are of regulation Civil War pattern, and the colonel obviously favours the heavy Civil War sabre rather than the light cavalry officers' model recently introduced. Soldiers have always collected souvenirs, and the colonel's choice here is a Sioux frame saddle.

G3 Sergeant Major, Full Dress, 4th U.S. Cavalry, 1876

Dress uniform for the sergeant major was the same as for enlisted cavalrymen. Cords and tassels on the helmet are of yellow mohair; the helmet cord is worn over the shoulder strap, with the end loop fastened to the button of the shoulder strap. The sabre is the Civil War model, not replaced as was the officers' sabre by this time. The service stripes on the lower part of the sleeves indicate one wartime and one peacetime enlistment. The coat is single-breasted, as opposed to the double-breasted full dress coat of officers (see plate F3), with eight buttons. Note also the yellow piping on the skirt, not worn by the officers. This is the regiment famous for General Custer's disastrous battle at Little Big Horn.

H1 Lieutenant-Colonel, 1st U.S. Volunteer Rough Riders, 1898

America's first volunteer regiment of cavalry was raised to augment the regular army facing overwhelming Spanish odds in Cuba. There was only one Lieutenant-Colonel of the regiment, and the temptation to portray Theodore Roosevelt has not been resisted. Largely a result of Roosevelt's personal enthusiasm, 'Teddy's Terrors' captured the imagination of the American public. Roosevelt is shown in his khaki cotton uniform with the well-known flamboyant addition of the blue polka-dot

kerchief round his neck. His shoulder loops bear lieutenant-colonel's 'leaves'. The blouse has a standing collar, bearing the 'U.S.V.' and cavalry insignia, five brass buttons, two breast pockets, and two skirt pockets with buttoned flaps.

H2 Trooper, 2nd U.S. Cavalry, 1917

A member of General Pershing's American Expeditionary Force in France, the Second Regiment were the only cavalry to go overseas. Their duties were mainly organizing remount stations for horses used by other divisions, notably the artillery. The First World War was the last major engagement in which the cavalry were mounted: the breeches, gaiters, and yellow hatcord, are the sole reminders of earlier days.

H3 Corporal Pathfinder, 1st Cavalry Division (Airmobile), 1967

The 1st Cavalry Division is basically an infantry division with the addition of 11th Aviation Group, designated as cavalry for historical reasons; and a major component of the Group is the Pathfinder section of which this corporal is a member. The Pathfinders control air traffic in forward area landing zones, and can parachute into an objective zone to mark landing areas. The uniform is standard jungle fatigues with extra carrying pockets, but service in Vietnam has thrown up a variety of improvised insignia and equipment. This man carries ammunition in a cloth bag intended to hold a claymore anti-personnel mine; he has substituted a general-purpose carrying strap on his M.16 rifle; and wears a survival knife which is authorized only for flying personnel. A black baseball cap and black scarf complete his personalized ensemble. The standard colour of 1st Division insignia is black on a drab olive background but there is a great variety of design and quality as they are often hand-made locally. Above his left pocket he wears the Combat Infantryman's Badge and, immediately below it, U.S. Airborne wings. The Pathfinder badge is worn on the left pocket, and Vietnamese Airborne wings, awarded for jumping with Vietnamese troops, above the right pocket. On his right sleeve is an 82nd Airborne Division patch indicating membership of that unit during the Dominican Republic Service; and a shield-shaped 1st Cavalry patch on the left sleeve cannot be seen.

INDEX

Figures in **bold** refer to illustrations.